Nathan
Comes to Town

by Johanna Biviano

illustrated by Cynthia Watts Clark

PEARSON

Scott
Foresman

Editorial Offices: Glenview, Illinois • Parsippany, New Jersey • New York, New York
Sales Offices: Needham, Massachusetts • Duluth, Georgia • Glenview, Illinois
Coppell, Texas • Ontario, California • Mesa, Arizona

ISBN: 0-328-13558-5

6 7 8 9 10 V0G1 14 13 12 11 10 09 08 07

CONTENTS

Chapter 1 The Big Fib

Adults always ask me the same question. "So, Drew, how's school going?"

I spend seven hours a day, five days a week, 40 weeks a year in school, why would I want to talk about it? I mean, how many kids do you know who want to talk about school? I think you would have to really love school to have a good answer to that annoying question.

I imagine myself saying, "Oh, school is incredible. I do really well at my studies. I'm a star athlete, too. The coaches beg me to play on all of their teams, but who has time with all of my volunteer work?" Instead, I find myself saying, "School's okay, Mr. Taylor."

He smiles and says, "You're in fifth grade, right? Do you have tons of homework?"

"Yup," I say, and Mr. Taylor chuckles. I wonder what's so funny about this.

Mr. Taylor tells me to "keep up the good work," and we get in the check-out line. I start to think of how I'm a big fibber.

Here's the fib: School is not okay. School is horrible. Every morning I wake up with this heavy feeling in my stomach, and I try to think of an excuse to stay home. My dad has heard them all by now, because I have two older sisters. He doesn't believe me for a second.

Every day I get on the school bus and sit by myself. I get to school, and all of the other kids talk and laugh, and I go straight to class. No one talks to me except for Ms. Krohner, and she says, "How are you today, Drew?"

I lie to her, too. "I'm fine, Ms. Krohner," I say and get out my homework.

The whole morning I try to listen, do my school work, and ignore all of the people ignoring me. I usually drift into daydreams about Dad getting a job in Bangladesh, moving the whole family, and starting at a new school. At around 11:00 A.M. I start to get hungry, just like everyone else, but then by the time lunch rolls around I feel sick.

I speed walk to the cafeteria, trying to get to the front of the crowd, so I can find a table in the corner. If I'm even a little bit late, there's no place for me to sit without asking the kids at that table, and they always look at me like I'm an alien.

There's one space at Soraya Klein's table, but the whole table is full of girls. She's really nice, but I don't want to be the one guy at the girls' table.

Luis Muniz's table has one seat open too. It's right next to Jeff McIntire, though, so I definitely can't sit there. To begin with, Luis is too cool for someone like me. But the real problem is Jeff. He used to kind of be a friend, but ever since the beginning of the school year, he treats me like dirt. He sneers at me, makes mean comments, and . . .

"Drew?" My dad says my name again. He's loading the bags from the shopping cart into the trunk of our car and has been trying to get my attention. "Can you help, please?"

I help him load the last two bags. "Are you okay, Drew?" He asks.

"Yeah, I'm okay," I say, lying again.

"Well, let's get home. It's getting late, and you've got an early day at school tomorrow."

"Don't remind me," I mutter, and we head home.

Chapter 2 Howdy, Neighbor!

"Hey guys," Julie says, launching herself out the front door, eager to help bring in groceries. "Let me get that heavy ol' bag for you, Daddykins!"

Dad stands frozen, staring at Julie skeptically. She bounds back into the house, arms full.

"She wants something," he says to me. I nod and wonder.

After Julie helps with the groceries, she gets Dad an iced tea, offers him a comfy spot on the couch, and hands him every remote control in the house. "I think there's a game on," she suggests.

"Okay, Julie," he says. "I give up. What's the big deal?"

"You got an interesting phone call, Dad," she says.

"I did, eh?"

"You did." She's smiling widely, a sneaky twinkle in her eye. "From Mrs. Shearer."

"The woman from the beach?" Dad asks, surprised.

"Yes, indeedy. Those people who had the hotel room next to us."

I remember the Shearer family. They had a kid, Nathaniel, who was almost my age and really smart. In fact, he was annoyingly smart. Nice but irritating at the same time, if you know what I mean. Anyway, Nathaniel had two older brothers. They were about my sisters' ages. Somehow everyone would run off together on that vacation, and I would end up with Nathaniel, like I was a babysitter or something.

Nathaniel's idea of a good time was to look up words in the dictionary. I remember looking up the words *dreary, tedious,* and *irksome,* which all pretty much mean "bored out of my mind," but he just didn't get it. He just said, "That's very interesting," and he would write down the word in his little black book.

When I would talk to him about some of my favorite basketball teams or players, he would give me a blank look. About the only thing we did the whole time was play chess. Of course, the little genius beat me most of the time.

"That was nice of Mrs. Shearer to call," my dad says, "Did she leave a message?"

"She left news, actually! They're moving here, and Patrick will be going to our school!" The light of understanding comes into my father's eyes. Julie hastens to add, "They'll all be going to school here."

"It'll be nice to see them again," Dad says pleasantly.

"Dad, please! It'll be awesome! So I thought maybe we could help them move in, and we could have a dinner party for them, and we could all sit together and talk! The kids," she looks at me, "can eat in the kitchen."

My dad gives Julie a warning look and opens his mouth to say something when Maura walks in. Maura's a senior in high school, and Dad trusts her to watch over us. She's my favorite sister, if I get to pick one.

"Hey Dad," she says, "Julie tells me her lover boy is moving into the neighborhood."

Julie blushes and makes an offended sound. "Hey, Mike Shearer is your age, if I remember correctly, and I think he likes you.

"He likes me in a swimsuit," says Maura, laughing. "Hey," she says to me, "Isn't that other kid your age? He seemed friendly."

"Yeah," I say. "He's a grade below."

Maura looks at me for a second, thoughtful. "It could be cool to have him around, eh Drew? I mean, he could be a good friend, don't you think?"

Dad laughs and says, "He's already got Jeff. I don't know how the Shearer kid would keep up." Dad knows Jeff can be a troublemaker, but he thinks that we are still friends.

I've been meaning to have a father-to-son talk with him about what happened between Jeff and me, but I already know what he will say. *Drew, you don't need friends like that,* and *I never really liked Jeff.* Last summer Jeff and I borrowed some of my dad's tools to build a fort. I don't know what happened, but some of the tools came up missing. When Dad asked Jeff about them, he acted like he didn't know what he was talking about. I just can't bring myself to tell him what happened.

"Ooh, Dad," Julie moans, excited again. "Didn't Drew tell you about the thing with Uncle Ray's basketball?" She gets so much pleasure out of my misery. All the better in her eyes, if public humiliation is involved.

"Tell me what?" Dad says to Julie. I take this as my cue to leave. By the time he turns to ask me this question, I am gone.

"Drew," my Dad says again as I am making my way up the stairs to my bedroom.

"Andrew! Come down here, please!" he commands. I stand still on the step, listening to Maura murmuring something to Dad. Finally, Dad says, "Jeff said that? That's awful! I never liked that kid. Why didn't Drew tell me?"

I continue up the stairs until I reach the safe haven of my room and shut the door behind me. Now I have a knot in my stomach. Just thinking about school sometimes make me ill.

Chapter 3 The New Kid in Class

"Yo, Drew. Wait up!"

Nathaniel can't see me rolling my eyes, so I go ahead and roll them. I can hear his sneakers slapping at the wet sidewalk and all the stuff in his backpack jostling as he closes in. I don't wait up, but he catches up with me anyway.

"Hey, Drew. What's up?" he asks, panting a little, making his short legs stretch to match my stride.

"Just going to the land of suffering, the same as every other day you ask me 'what's up,'" I say, ruder than I meant to be.

"You mean school, right?" I don't answer him. "But today is not like every other day, Drew."

I look him in the eye for the first time. Nathaniel is so small, even for a fourth grader. When he first started at our school two days ago, I was sure he would get beat up or something. So far, he seems happy to go to school every morning. That thought is novel to me.

The bus rolls up before he can tell me why today is so special. I try to let him get on first, so I can sit far, far away from whatever seat he chooses. He bows gallantly and says, "No, I insist, you first."

He's still bowing as I roll my eyes, so he doesn't see it this time, either.

On the bus, Nathaniel bounces down next to me before I'm even sitting in my seat.

"So, like I was saying . . ." he begins.

"Yeah? What's so special about today? Are they letting you eat the finger paint in fourth grade art?" Even as I say it, I'm ashamed of how mean I can be.

Nathaniel laughs. "I wouldn't know," he says, "because I'm not in the fourth grade anymore."

"That's unbelievable," I say. "They demoted you to kindergarten? You should sic your mom on the principal!"

"No! No, Drew!" He's so excited. I know what's coming. That familiar foreboding fills my stomach. "I'm in your class now!"

"You mean you're in fifth grade?" I ask, incredulous.

"Not only in fifth grade, I'm in your class, Ms. Krohner's class. My teacher had me take a test, and they said I'd be bored in fourth grade."

"Wow," I say. Nathaniel looks at me expectantly. All I can think is that having this little genius kid following me around for the rest of the year is guaranteed to make this bad year even worse.

While I ponder, Nathaniel babbles on. "It'll be so cool. I mean, it's hard moving to a new school, but now I have a friend in my class! How perfect is that? You can show me around and introduce me to your friends. Protect me from the big bad kids. Ha!" He thinks he is joking about this.

He keeps talking. "When I met you this summer, I thought to myself, 'He's a good guy.' And now we're at the same school!"

At school, Ms. Krohner takes a moment out of her strict schedule just long enough to introduce Nathaniel. She doesn't explain that he has the biggest, fiercest brain anyone has ever seen and should be in college already. Nathaniel smiles shyly at the class and finds a seat.

Looking around the room I notice that everyone is curious about this little kid, especially Jeff. I can only see his profile, but he has a wicked look in his eye. I realize that Jeff really is a big bad kid, and Nathaniel may need some protection. He might not get it from me, though.

All morning I feel like I can't get rid of Nathaniel. Ms. Krohner has us work together on a social studies project. As we read through a newspaper and find the cities on a map, Nathaniel seems to find everything lightning fast. He raises his hand constantly to ask questions, and Ms. Krohner doesn't seem annoyed at all. I notice Jeff is letting Luis do all the work in their group, and every once in a while I can feel him staring at me. I look up to catch him smiling at me with that same wicked look in his eye.

In gym class, Coach Johnson asks me to demonstrate dribbling to Nathaniel on the basketball court. He may be smart, but he can't dribble to save his life! I try to keep my temper and not draw attention to us.

Suddenly, the ball bounces out of Nathaniel's grasp and heads straight in between Jeff and Luis, hitting their ball and sending them running after it. Nathaniel runs after our ball happily and yells, "Sorry about that!" Luis nods a little and goes back to practicing lay-ups.

I feel Jeff's stare again. I know that look. Lunchtime comes all too quickly.

Chapter 4 One Lousy Lunch

I'm way at the front of the class, rushing to lunch as usual, when I hear Nathaniel calling me from the back of the group. "Hey, Drew! Wait up!"

I can't wait up! Even if I wanted to sit with him, there wouldn't be two seats together if we take our sweet time getting to the cafeteria. I rush to find myself a seat in the corner and try to become invisible.

Nathaniel enters the room, looking like a tiny elf in a forest of big fifth graders. He looks lost. I watch him as he looks around, deciding where to sit. His eyes light up, and he waves to someone, heading forward like he's found a friend. I look to see where he's waving.

Soraya Klein makes some room at her table, smiling and talking with Nathaniel. He doesn't seem bothered by the fact that he's surrounded by girls. He plops his lunch bag on the table and digs in.

I get a weird feeling, watching him hanging out with Soraya. It takes a few seconds, but all at once I know what that feeling is: envy.

"Ha ha ha... Even that little first grader has friends to sit with!" The leering voice behind me comes from Jeff McIntire, of course. I know better than to talk back. It's usually easier if I just keep quiet and wait for the interaction to be over.

"Looks like he's movin' in on your girlfriend, Drewypoo!" Some kids at his table laugh loudly and make kissing noises. My face gets hot. He knows Soraya isn't my girlfriend. He just wants to get to me.

"You might as well give in and sit with them. Hey, you could bring your girly basketball! You could talk to them about the pretty color and everything." The guys sitting with Jeff just stare at me waiting to see what I'll do. This is worse than going to the dentist to have him fill a mouthful of cavities.

I try to look busy peeling the crusts off of my sandwich. I can't bring myself to eat it. Even when Jeff goes back to his lunch, I just sit there, poking at my food.

By the time the buses pull up in front of school I'm panicking. Do I have to take the bus home with Nat the Gnat? (That nickname suits him—he's like a pesky insect.) I practically run out the school doors, the Gnat is right behind me.

"Hey Drew!" he calls to me. By now I know the next line: "Wait up!"

Right then, the whole horrible day catches up with me. How does this kid miss the message that I don't want him hanging around? Life is hard enough with Jeff breathing down my neck, my quiz grades slipping because of daydreaming, and endless days of isolated lunches. I stop in my tracks and turn to the little kid jumbling after me with a big stupid smile on his face.

"Look, Gnat," I say, nearly shouting, "I am so sick of you following me around. Leave me *alone*!"

The smile leaks from his face as he catches his breath from running. "But, Drew, I thought we were friends."

"You thought wrong, you little insect!"

I turn my back on Nathaniel and hurry to find a seat. I try to stare straight in front of me, but I can't help it, my gaze drifts to find Nathaniel in the crowd. He's almost unrecognizable without a smile on his face.

I watch as Soraya approaches him. Our eyes meet for an instant, and her face turns cold. She turns back to Nathaniel and smiles, then heads off to her bus.

Nathaniel doesn't look up as he walks down the aisle of the bus and takes the first open seat. My heart won't stop pounding. My face won't cool down.

I'm the big bad kid.

Chapter 5 Dinner for Two?

Later, I'm hiding in my room, trying to push that awful feeling out of my stomach with homework and getting nowhere. I found myself staring at the same math problem for what seemed like an hour. Sometimes I wish that life could be more like math—there's only one right answer. Unfortunately, life seems to be more like a maze; you run around in circles, not really sure about where you're going.

About an hour later, I smell something strange. I find Julie desperately waving at billows of smoke coming from the open oven.

"Whoa, Julie, are you cooking or is this a science project gone wrong?"

"Very funny, Drew," she says.

The smoke alarm starts beeping urgently, and Julie yells at me, "Help! Do something!"

I run in to close the oven door, turn off the oven, and turn on the overhead fan. I open the kitchen window. The alarm stops ringing after a couple of frantic minutes.

"Phew... Thanks, little bro," says Julie.

Maura comes thumping down the stairs just as Julie opens the oven and lets out a fresh cloud of smoke, setting the alarm off again. This time Maura helps by reaching up to the alarm and loosening the battery.

"Oooh, Maura," I say, "you're not supposed to do that!"

"It's a quick fix," she says. "Remind me to put it back!" This is the moment, of course, when Dad walks in the front door.

"Yum yum," he says, "nothin' like the smell of home cookin'!" He walks into the kitchen, takes one look at the whole group of us, and zeroes in on Julie.

"Well, Jules?" He stands expectantly, setting his keys down on the table.

"Hiya Dad. We have guests for dinner."

"The city's Fire Squad?" he asks, as he pushed the battery of the smoke alarm back in place.

"Oh, Daddy, you're so funny," Julie says, laughing nervously. "The Shearers, Dad! Remember when you said we could have a dinner party," she says, her face hopeful."Good grief," my dad says, and then he and Julie have a discussion while Maura and I sneak away. Eventually, we discover that the Shearers think they are invited to come over at six o'clock, for a roast turkey dinner. Julie throws out her failed cooking attempt, and Dad orders three large pizzas. Maura and I look for chairs for all eight of us.

As Maura and I lug folding chairs from the basement, Julie suddenly starts whining at us, "No, no, not in the dining room! Those two can go in the kitchen, 'cause that's where Nathaniel and Drew will eat.

"Oh no you don't." My dad's voice reverberates from inside the oven, where he's scraping at something from Julie's cooking mishap.

Maura looks at my flushed face and panicked eyes and considers the situation.

"I dunno, Dad," she says. "Maybe the boys should get to know each other."

And to think she was my favorite sister.

Chapter 6 Uncle Ray's Basketball

The doorbell rings promptly at six o'clock, and everything's a blur of politeness. Nathaniel hardly looks at me as Mrs. Shearer and Dad talk about how lucky it is that Nathaniel ended up in a class with a friend.

"Thanks for looking out for Nat," says Mrs. Shearer. "Kids can be such bullies these days." I can't look her in the eye as I think of Nathaniel telling his mom about his great day at school.

The pizza arrives moments later. With Julie batting her eyelashes at Patrick, and Mike staring at Maura, I'm almost glad to escape to the kitchen. But, of course, Nathaniel has to sit there, too.

"I'm not feeling hungry, Mom," he says, worry coming through in his voice.

"Me either," I mutter.

Dad overhears me and says, "Well then, why don't you guys go out and shoot some hoops? Come in when you're hungry." I shrug and head out the door.

In the driveway, I dribble the infamous purple basketball my Uncle Ray had given me at the end of the summer. Nathaniel studies his shoelaces.

"Hey, Nathaniel, want a shot?" He scrambles to catch the ball. He tries a lay-up and misses. "I should have warned you," I say. "This basketball is cursed."

"Really?" he asks, still untrusting.

"Well, I thought it was supercool when my Uncle Ray gave it to me, but I haven't had anything but terrible luck since it arrived," I explain.

Just to prove it, I shoot. And miss, of course. The ball rolls off under the neighbors' shrubs. Nathaniel runs after the ball. He looks like he wants to say something.

"Yeah," I say. "It's funny because my uncle wanted me to have this basketball so badly—for good luck! Partly because he saw me and Jeff playing basketball all last summer."

I kept talking. "Anyway, when the ball arrived I took it to school with me, and I guess the timing was bad. Jeff was trying to impress these guys from the grade above, and that cool kid Luis was hanging out with him. I passed Jeff the ball right in front of them, and I guess the combination of stuff was too much. He was embarrassed to be associated with me, and he thought the color of the basketball was sissy. So he laid into me with all kinds of insults and nasty comments."

"*That's* why you're not friends?"

"Yep, up until the beginning of school Jeff and I would hang out in the neighborhood. Then he just turned on me because of this stupid basketball, and it's been a really bad year since then."

"No wonder you stay away from him."

"Yeah. He wanted me to act like he was doing me a favor being my friend or else he didn't want anything to do with me. I guess he thinks other kids think I am a loser."

"He doesn't sound like a nice guy."

"He *could* be nice," I say, catching Nathaniel's pass, "He just stopped."

"He seems to be nice to that kid Luis," observed Nathaniel.

"Yeah. Jeff thinks Luis is the coolest kid in the whole school."

"He might be," says Nathaniel. "But you know Luis doesn't think you're a loser."

"He doesn't?" I ask in disbelief.

"Neither does Soraya. She thinks you're pretty cool." A huge tension in my back releases. I feel like I am breathing for the first time in months. Maybe things aren't as bad as I thought they were. I dribble the basketball, shoot it at the basket, and it goes in.

I smile at Nathaniel. "Nat, I am sorry I was acting like a huge jerk the other day. I just couldn't deal."

Nathaniel smiles a little. "So, do you want to be friends? 'Cause I could use a few friends."

Before he could keep rambling on, I interrupt him. "Yeah, Nate. It would be cool to hang out with you."

He gives me big smile. "Excellent!" It feels much better giving him a nice nickname. And it's a relief to see him smiling and know that I am not making *him* feel like he's a loser.

"I'm getting hungry," I say. "How about you?"

Three Who Overcame

Marian Anderson: Growing up in South Philadelphia, Marian Anderson was forced to quit school at 13 years old to help support her family. Anderson eventually got enough support from her community to take singing lessons with a professional opera singer. Enjoying instant praise from all for her voice, she still had to wait until 1955 for her first performance at the Metropolitan Opera House in New York. She was the first African American to perform there.

Albert Einstein: At 15 years old, Albert Einstein rebelled against his high school teachers' authority. He had such a bad attitude that he was asked to leave the school midterm! Although he excelled at mathematics, physics, and sciences in general, he failed the arts portion of his entrance exam for the Swiss Federal Institute of Technology. This rebel drop-out went on to become the world renowned physicist who developed the theory of relativity—a theory students of science continue to debate today!

Amy Van Dyken: At the closing ceremonies of the 1996 Olympic Games in Atlanta, Georgia, Amy Van Dyken proudly displayed four gold medals for swimming. Who could have expected such a victory from a girl who couldn't participate in gym class in her childhood? Van Dyken had severe asthma and started swimming to strengthen her lungs. After years of hard practice and determination, this self-proclaimed "nerd" set records, becoming the first American woman to win four gold medals in one Olympic year.